American English Expressions

By Gabriel F. Gargiulo

American English Expressions

Copyright 2014 by Gabriel F. Gargiulo

American English Expressions

Table of Contents

Introduction　　　　　4

Expressions　　　　　5

Index　　　　　44

For Further Reading　　　52

American English Expressions

Introduction

New expressions are coming into American English every day. They are invented by the media, or used on a TV program, and within days millions of people are using them. Other expressions have been part of the language for a long time, but are hard to understand when taken literally. The world of business has its own form of office jargon that you need to understand if you are working in the USA. This book contains 158 of these expressions and gives their equivalent in standard English, as well as examples of how they are used.

We have included strange, incomprehensible "words" such as "529" and "401(K)." I have never been able to understand how anyone could use a number instead of a name, or a paragraph number in a book in place of a name. I am told that if I look in the huge book of American tax laws, that paragraph number 401, with subheading "K" I will find a definition of a "401(K)." I'll put that on my bucket list.

All the expressions are listed in the Index at the back of the book. This book is intended for someone whose first language is not American English. My years of teaching American English to the foreign-born have taught me that many people come to the United States speaking English well already, but they cannot understand many of the new expressions that they hear in daily life or on TV, that they read in the newspapers or on websites. We wish you luck and hope that you will derive as much pleasure from foreign languages as we do teaching them.

Gabe Gargiulo

American English Expressions

1040 — income tax declaration form.
1040 is the number of the standard IRS form for declaring income. You don't "submit" the completed form to the IRS, you "file" it. In IRS language you "file your 1040," but in normal English you "submit your tax declaration."
Example:
I'm almost finished with my **1040**, I'm going to file it soon.

1099 — income tax declaration form.
1099 is the number of an IRS form. Every business that pays money for services sends this to the IRS.
Example:
Here is your **1099** for the money that we paid you last year.

401(K) — retirement savings plan.
A government-approved plan that allows you to save money for retirement. Named after the chapter in the tax law code in which it is defined.
Example:
I'm putting $100 a month into my **401(K)**.

529 — a savings plan to pay college expenses.
A government-approved plan that allows you to save money for your children's college expenses.
Example:
I put $100 a month into my children's **529**.

American English Expressions

6 figure income — income between $100,000 and $999,999.
An income which needs 6 numerical digits to write it.
Example:
I can't get a **6 figure income** as a greeter at the local Mart.

A couple a three — two, three, or more.
This is an outdated expression, but I heard it recently.
Example:
Let's go get **a couple a three** beers.

Aggro — aggravation, annoyance.
Example:
I'm not going to work today. I don't need the **aggro**.

All walks of life — all income levels, all occupations, all backgrounds.
Example:
I went to the auto races and there were people there from **all walks of life**.

Apples and oranges — a comparison that doesn't make sense.
Example:
How do you like it in Mississippi compared to New York City?
That's **apples and oranges**.

American English Expressions

At the end of the day — when all is said and done, to sum it up.
Example:
Joe, you make a lot of sales calls, but **at the end of the day** you are just not selling enough vacuum cleaners.

Back-to-back — consecutive. One after another, with no interruption.
Back-to-back is really not the same as consecutive, but this is the way that it is used.
Example:
I'll be busy all day Monday — I have 4 classes **back-to-back**.

Bad optics — embarrassing photos.
Example:
The candidate withdrew his name from the race because of some really **bad optics**.

Ballpark figure — unfounded approximation.
Same as "Off the top of your head." Someone needs a quick answer to a complex question, and doesn't want to wait for you to figure out the answer correctly. You are expected to give an answer that will be taken seriously and reported to upper management and/or the media.
Example:
I need a **ballpark figure** — how many people do we have working in New York?

American English Expressions

Beam me up Scotty! — These people are nuts, get me out of here!
Example:
This UFO conference is unbelievable — **beam me up Scotty!**

Begs the question — assuming that your conclusion is true before proving it.
Circular reasoning. "Proving" that something is true by assuming it is true.
This is often used incorrectly to mean "that makes me want to ask the question."
Examples:
It's raining because the weather is bad.
Prices are rising because of inflation. (Rising prices = inflation.)
I didn't steal it, officer, I'm an honest person.

Bet you did! — OK, but I don't believe it!
"I bet you did!" really means "Oh yeah? I don't think so."
Example:
Hello, mom, I shaved off my beard and took the nose rings out.
I bet you did!

Big whoop! — that's really great! (Sarcastically.)
This is like saying "Wow, that's really great!" and not meaning it.
Example:
They're going to give me a $.25 cent per hour raise. **Big whoop!**

American English Expressions

Blah blah — meaningless talking.
Example:
Congressman Blather was talking about how he was going to help us, and **blah blah**.

Blow the whistle — tell the authorities about a crime.
Example:
He **blew the whistle** on his boss's illegal actions. (He revealed his boss's illegal actions to the legal authorities.)

Blue state — a state whose electoral votes were for a Democrat in the last presidential election.
Example:
Connecticut and Massachusetts are **blue states**.

Bone up — do a last-minute preparation.
Example:
My exam in Chemistry is tomorrow. I've got to **bone up**.

Brain freeze — ice cream headache.
What happens when you eat too much ice cream too fast.
Example:
I ate ice cream too fast. I have **brain freeze**.

American English Expressions

Brain surgery — very difficult, requiring much intelligence.
Example:
Did you figure out how to use your new computer? It's not **brain surgery**. It's not difficult.

Brush up — do a last-minute preparation.
Example:
My exam in Chemistry is tomorrow. I've got to **brush up**.

Bucket list — a list of things that you want to do before you die.
This comes from the expression "kick the bucket" (die.)
Example:
On my **bucket list** are: see Stonehenge, the Grand Canyon, the Taj Mahal and Machu Picchu.

Bull session — long-winded discussion.
Example:
Come in, we're having a **bull session**. Come in, we're having a long-winded discussion.

American English Expressions

Butt dialing — when your cell phone dials a number that you didn't intend to dial.
Generally this is because the phone is in your pocket and a button is pressed without your knowing it.
Example:
I **butt dialed** my boss and she heard me saying that I was looking for another job, so now I'm toast.

Butt out! — this does not concern you!
See also *Mind your business.*
Example:
My wife and I are having a discussion. **Butt out!**

Cakewalk — an easy task.
Example:
Walking across Niagara Falls on a steel cable is no **cakewalk**.

Can't make this up — incredible, but true.
Example:
A man was struck by lightning 7 times in the same place. He survived. You **can't make this up**.

American English Expressions

Carbon footprint — how much carbon dioxide is released into the atmosphere.
Example:
Solar panels have a **carbon footprint** when they are first manufactured, but make up for it after 2-3 years of use.

Catch as catch can — without a plan, haphazardly.
Impossible to analyze this expression. It can't be taken literally.
Example:
Welcome to the first day of class. The desks haven't arrived yet, so it's **catch as catch can**.

Chapter 11 — bankruptcy.
This means the company is in bankruptcy proceedings. The name "Chapter 11" comes from the place where it is described in a book, known as the US Bankruptcy code. It is found in Chapter 11. This is like saying that Bill and Sue are in "Matthew Chapter 5, Verse 32." (A verse about committing adultery.)
Example:
The company is in **Chapter 11**. Don't plan on buying any stock.

Chill out! — calm down!
Example:
Hey, don't get excited, **chill out** man! Sorry I wrecked your Camaro.

American English Expressions

Cloud computing — using a program on a web server.
Your computer uses the Internet to connect to a remote computer which contains the program that is being used, and your data that it is processing. With "Cloud" computing, you do not need to buy the program and you do not need to worry about losing your data when your home computer crashes. With non-cloud computing, the program being used is on your computer, along with the data.
Example :
Many companies furnish **cloud computing** services to their customers.

Clueless — completely unaware, uninformed.
Example:
Joe's wife is cheating on him, but he's **clueless**.

Cocooning — staying home more and more.
Example:
Because of the high price of gasoline, we're **cocooning** a lot.

Coed, or co-ed — a college that admits both men and women.
It also means a woman who attends college or school.
Example:
Most colleges today are **co-ed**.

American English Expressions

Cold is the new hot — use cold water to wash clothes.
Only an advertising agency could invent an expression like this. Unfortunately, many other advertisers have started using variations of this expression.
Example:
Cold is the new hot. Tea is the new coffee. Green is the new blue. Orange is the new turquoise. And so on, without end.

Cold turkey — suddenly, without help.
Example:
He stopped smoking **cold turkey**. (He stopped smoking immediately, on the spot.)

Come unhinged — lose control of one's emotions.
Example:
My wife **came unhinged** when I told her that I was going to Cancun with my secretary on a business trip.

Comeback Kid — someone who achieves success after many failures.
They thought he was finished, but he made a recovery.
Example:
I thought his career was finished, but he's the **Comeback Kid**.

American English Expressions

Computer glitch — human error blamed on the computer.
Whenever an employee of a business makes a mistake while writing a computer program or while using a computer in some way, the company attributes it to a "computer glitch," thinking that the public will be impressed by the word "computer" and accept the explanation.
This is sometimes called a "computer snafu."
Example:
We are genuinely sorry for the inconvenience caused by our posting your names, addresses, dates of birth, annual income, mother's maiden names, social security numbers, ATM card PINS, and dog's vaccination history on a public webpage. It was a "**computer glitch**."

Con man — someone who deceives you.
Example:
Bernard Madoff was a **con man**.

Cookie-cutter — all the same.
Example:
He lives in a row of **cookie-cutte**r houses. The houses all look the same.

Co-pay or copay — you pay.
The part of a doctor's, dentist's or pharmacist's bill that you pay, which the insurance doesn't pay.
Example:
Your **co-pay** for your brain transplant is $41,000. You owe us $41,000 for your brain transplant.

American English Expressions

Could care less — it's not important to me.
Also, "I couldn't care less" means the same thing.
See also *Meh*.
Example:
What do you think about your competitor going out of business?
I **could care less**!

Crickets — silence.
Example:
They asked the politician about his illegal contributions from special interest groups. The answer? **Crickets**.

Deal-breaker — an unacceptable condition.
A deal-breaker is the one item that you cannot accept, and which makes you refuse a deal or a sale.
Examples:
I was offered a job with good pay and benefits, but it's in Detroit, and that's a **deal-breaker**.
I wanted the new phone, but the $400 price tag was a **deal-breaker**.

Diddly — nothing.
Short for diddly squat.
See also *Jack* and *Zero, zip, zilch*.
Examples:
Did you win anything in the lottery? — **Diddly**!
You don't know **diddly** about playing the lottery.

American English Expressions

Do not call list — a list of telephone numbers which telemarketers are not allowed to phone.
Example:
The members of Congress gave themselves an exemption from the law on the "**do not call list**."
My phone is on the **do not call list**, but I got a call from congressman Nuthatch anyway.

Do you mind? — Does it annoy you?
Does this bother you?
Example:
Do you mind if I smoke? No, **I don't mind**. Go ahead and smoke.

Don't just talk the talk, walk the walk. — Don't just talk about what you believe, show your beliefs through your actions.
People also say "Walk the talk."
Example:
You talk about adopting abandoned animals, but will you **walk the walk and not just talk the talk**?

Done deal — the decision has already been made, favorably.
Something that's a done deal is something you can count on. It has already been decided, favorably.
Example:
I applied for the promotion and it looks like a **done deal**.

American English Expressions

Drive-by shooting — shooting from a car.
A gang member in a car shoots someone who is walking on the sidewalk, and speeds away.
Example:
Someone was killed today in a **drive-by shooting**.

Drop a dime — make a phone call.
At one time, the price of a phone call at a pay phone was 10 cents, or one dime.
Example:
I haven't heard from you. **Drop a dime** sometime.

Drunk as a skunk — really drunk.
Example:
Joe came back from the party **drunk as a skunk**, and smelling like one too.

Duck soup — an easy task.
Example:
Sure I'll fix your transmission — it's **duck soup**.

American English Expressions

Easy does it! — slowly. Relax.
This means "be careful," "do it slowly."
See also *Take it easy.*
Example:
Easy does it when moving a large sofa.

Food pantry — free food for the needy.
Example:
There's a **food pantry** every Tuesday in the center of town. My neighbor goes there every week.

Foodie — gourmet.
Example:
Joe is a real **foodie**. He likes all kinds of food.

Free range — animals that are not confined while they are being raised.
Example:
This Thanksgiving we're eating **free range** Turkey. We feel better knowing the turkey was able to roam free before being slaughtered for our table.

American English Expressions

From the get-go — from the very beginning.
You can say "git-go" too.
Example:
My boss and I didn't get along **from the get-go**.

Fuhgeddaboutit! — forget about it!
A New York City expression.
Example:
Do you think they will be picking up the trash today? **Fuhgeddaboutit!**

Game-changer — an overriding condition that makes all other conditions irrelevant.
All other aspects of the situation are unimportant. The game-changer is the only one that is needed for me to make my decision.
Examples:
I would like to buy that house, but it's next to a windmill, and that's a **game-changer**.
I didn't want a dog until I went to the animal shelter with a friend and Rover started licking my hand. That was a real **game-changer**.

Gang-banger — member of a criminal gang.
Example:
Don't associate with him. He's a **gang-banger**.

American English Expressions

Generation X — people born in the 60's and 70's.
Name created by the media to describe people born in the 60's and 70's. The name was created so as to attempt to describe each individual as having common characteristics.
Example:
I'm a **generation X**'er. According to the stereotype I'm lazy and unmotivated.

Generation Y — people born in the 80's.
According to the stereotype, generation Y'ers are narcissistic and knowledgeable in electronics.
Example:
I'm a **generation Y**'er, so why don't I have an iPhone?

Get on the bandwagon — doing what other people are doing because they are doing it.
Following a crowd and doing what the crowd does without thinking whether it is a good idea or not. Uncritical group thinking. Irrational, unthinking conformity.
Example:
Everybody else is getting a smartphone, so you had better **get on the bandwagon** and get one too.

Go Dutch — each one pays for his/her portion at a restaurant.
You can also say "Dutch treat."
Example:
Let's eat at the Waldorf Astoria. We'll **go Dutch**.

American English Expressions

Good riddance! — I'm happy that it is gone.
Example:
Ben Laden is gone! **Good riddance!**

Got your back — watching out for you.
Example:
Nothing to worry about, Joe, **I've got your back**.

Haul ass — work very hard.
Example:
Welcome to the project team, Joe, the project is late and we've got to **haul ass**.

High on the hog — eating rich foods or living a rich life.
Example:
Since Joe won the lottery he's living **high on the hog**.

Hit the ground running — work like an experienced person on the first day of the job.
Paratroopers hope to reach the ground in one piece, and in good enough condition to start fighting immediately. That is the original meaning of the expression.
Example:
We need someone for the job who must be able to **hit the ground running**. The applicant must be able to get to work right away without any training and act like an expert at once because the company is not going to train him/her.

American English Expressions

Hitting on — unwanted flirting.
Example:
Joe got fired because he was always **hitting on** his co-worker Sally.

Hump day — Wednesday.
"Hump" is the hardest part of a job. After the hump, it gets easier.
See also *Over the hump.*
Example:
Oh good, it's Wednesday — **hump day**.

I wouldn't put it past him. — I would not be surprised if he did it.
I know what he is like. I know that he is capable of doing this.
Example:
Joe is accused of stealing from his company. **I wouldn't put it past him**.

I'm good. — I don't need anything else.
Example:
Would you like some more soda? — No, **I'm good**.

I'm like totally there. — I'm enthusiastic about that.
Example:
Do you like Kim Kardashian? — Yeah, like man, **I'm like totally there**. (Translation: I am excited about her.)

American English Expressions

Inhale food — eat fast.
Example:
You really **inhaled** the Tiramisù.

It is what it is! — you have to accept it the way that it is, and you can't change it.
Example:
I lost my job and the credit card company wants a payment. **It is what is is!**

Jack — nothing.
Short for jack shit.
See also *Diddly* and *Zero, zip, zilch.*
Example:
Did you win anything in the lottery? — I didn't win **jack**!

John Hancock — signature.
John Hancock was one of the people who signed the Declaration of Independence. Now his name is used for any signature.
Example:
Can I have your **John Hancock** on this loan application?

Jumped the shark — to be no longer useful.
Example:
The Euro has really **jumped the shark**.

American English Expressions

Just sayin' — that's only my opinion, don't be offended.
Example:
Sally, you really look fat in that dress. **Just sayin'**.

Kitchen sink — everything, including some odd, unexpected things.
The original expression was "Everything but the kitchen sink." "They sold everything but the kitchen sink". Then people started saying "kitchen sink" meaning "everything."
Examples:
The house burned down and everything was lost but the **kitchen sink**.
Try my new **kitchen sink** cookies — they have everything in them but the **kitchen sink**.

Labor of love — what you do because you love it, not for money.
Example:
Sally's book on Alzheimer's is a **labor of love**.

American English Expressions

Leap tall buildings — perform impossible tasks on the job.
Superman was able to jump over high buildings.
See also *Walk on water*.
Example:
The applicant for the job must be able to **leap tall buildings**. The applicant must be able to work harder and better than most mortals.

Learning curve — hard to learn.
Example:
I'm learning to be a brain surgeon. There's a **learning curve**.

Luck out — have good luck.
Example:
I **lucked out** — I bought the last generator in the store before the big storm.

Man up — be strong, act like a real man.
Example:
You've got to **man up** and take responsibility for your actions.

American English Expressions

Meh! — I don't care!
See also *Could care less.*
Example:
Kids, how would you like macaroni and cheese for dinner? — **Meh**!

Mind your business! — this does not concern you!
See also *Butt out.*
Example:
Yes, I'm smoking a cigar. **Mind your** own **business**!

Mirror image — exactly the same.
Example:
My secretary is a **mirror image** of Jennifer Lopez. My wife is jealous.

My bad — I said something untrue.
Example:
So, on your resume it says that you were CEO at GM. — **My bad**, I meant Gary's Motors.

Never mind — pay no attention.
Ignore it. Let it drop.
Examples:
Never mind the 800 pound gorilla behind you.
Joe, would you open this jar for me — No, I'm too busy. — Oh, **never mind**!

American English Expressions

Nitty-gritty — real important details.
Example:
The boss got down to the **nitty-gritty** of the situation during the staff meeting.

No big deal — not something important.
This often minimizes something that is really important.
Example:
The boss wants to see you Friday at 4; it's **no big deal**.

No-brainer — easy to understand.
Example:
Do high taxes on small businesses discourage growth? That's a **no-brainer**.

Off the top of your head! — quick, give me an answer!
Same as "Ballpark figure." Someone needs a quick answer to a complex question, and doesn't want to wait for you to figure out the answer correctly. You are expected to give an answer that will be taken seriously and reported to upper management and/or the media.
Example:
Off the top of your head, how many people do we have working in New York?

American English Expressions

On a roll — enjoying one success after another.
Example:
I just won two games of poker. I'm **on a roll**.

On steroids — very strong.
Example:
That tiger is like my cat **on steroids**.

On-the-job-training — starting a job without adequate training.
If you want this job you had better know how to do it, because we don't have time to teach you how to do it.
Example:
Great job! Great pay! **On-the-job-training**! Here's a job that no one wants. The salary is low. You had better know how to do it because we don't have time to train you.

Out there — really strange.
Example:
That new TV show is so **out there** — it's creepy.

Over the hump — finished with the most difficult part.
See also *Hump day.*
Example:
It's a hard job, but I'm **over the hump** now.

American English Expressions

Pencil in — write this on your calendar, but it's not definite.
Reserve a time on your appointment calendar, but it's not definite. You had better be there, even if I forget to confirm it.
Example:
Joe, **pencil in** the meeting for 7 AM Monday.

Pie hole — mouth.
Example:
Shut your **pie hole**! Shut your mouth!

Piece of cake — an easy task.
Example:
The math final exam was a **piece of cake**.

Piping hot — very hot.
Example:
The pie just came out of the oven, and it's **piping hot**.

Post mortem — discussion of a recent failure.
When a project fails, there is a meeting to discuss why the project failed and who is going to get fired.
Example:
The project blew up in our faces. The boss called a **post mortem** for Friday at 4 PM.

American English Expressions

Poster child — good example of something.
Example:
The movie star has become a **poster child** for plastic surgery.

Provider — doctor or hospital.
A person or institution that provides medical service, such as a doctor, dentist, hospital, medical laboratory or clinic.
Example:
You filled out your insurance form incorrectly. You forgot to include your **provider**.

Rain date — a date to which an event is (or may be) postponed.
It's not always because of rain.
Example:
We will have an outdoor picnic on the 21st. The **rain date** is the 28th.

Rank and file — the workers or employees. Not the management.
The people who do the work in an organization are the rank and file.
Example:
Management is happy over outsourcing, but the **rank and file** is upset over it.

American English Expressions

Red state — a state whose electoral votes were for a Republican in the last presidential election.
Example:
Texas and Alaska are **red states**.

Reverse 911 — telephone alert system.
A system that some cities use to alert residents of dangers such as fires and floods. Each resident receives a phone call that alerts to the danger.
Example:
If you want to be kept informed in case of natural disaster, you had better register your phone number with your town's **Reverse 911**.

Rocket science — very difficult, requiring much intelligence.
Example:
Did you figure out how to use your new computer? It's not **rocket science**. It's not difficult.

Rummage sale — sale of used items to raise money for a charity.
Example:
Can you come to my church hall? We're having a **rummage sale** today.

American English Expressions

Run that by me again! — repeat that!
After someone says something that is difficult to understand, or tries to explain a new or radical idea, you may say "Run that by me again!"
Example:
The square of the length of the hypotenuse is equal to the sum of the squares of the lengths of the other two sides. You then take the square root of your answer.
Run that by me again!

Run-around — bad customer service.
When you contact a company for customer service, and they make you wait, hang up and call back, call another number, talk to someone who can't help you, promise to call back and not do it, promise to give you a refund and not do it.
Example:
I tried to get the company to give me a refund for the defective merchandise, but all I got from customer service was the **run-around**.

Running late — already late.
Example:
I'm **running late** and I'm going to be late for our appointment, and the next one, and the one after that.

American English Expressions

Schedule C — the name of an IRS form.
In the arcane world of the IRS, "schedule" means "form."
Example:
Fill out **Schedule C**, and enter on line 5(a) the difference between line 23 and line 30 on schedule 1040 (but not form 1040-EZ) unless zero, in which case you need to file Schedule Xz-54h (unless your AGI is over $52,327, in which case figure your penalty on form Cx-65(b).)

Sea change — big change.
This has nothing to do with the sea changing.
Example:
The Voting Rights Law brought about a **sea change** in America.

Senior moment — temporary lapse of memory or attention.
Example:
For a minute I forgot my home phone number. I guess I had a **senior moment**.

Shoo-in — a guaranteed winner.
Example:
Joe is a **shoo-in** for the election. He is sure to win.

American English Expressions

Simpatico — getting along well.
This is pseudo-Spanish. Simpático in Spanish means nice, friendly.
Example:
I see you two are very **simpatico** - you two understand each other.

Sitting duck — easy target.
Example:
Walking home alone at midnight, I was a **sitting duck**.

Skin in the game — you can win, or you can lose what you invested.
Your own interests are at stake.
Example:
If the stock market goes up or down, I have no **skin in the game**.

Snowball in Hell (or snowball's chance in Hell) — very unlikely.
Example:
It's a **snowball's chance in Hell** that I will get that job in Paris.

American English Expressions

Sold a bill of goods — be cheated.
Buy something without verifying that it is real, valid and working.
Example:
I was **sold a bill of goods** on that used car. I was really cheated.

Sound bite — short recording of a person's words that is broadcast repeatedly on the media.
Example:
Everyone has heard the famous **sound bite** of John F. Kennedy: "Ask not what your country can do for you, ask what you can do for your country."

Soup kitchen — free meals for the homeless.
Example:
The homeless go to the **soup kitchen** every evening for a hot meal.

Staycation — Stay Close to Home Vacation.
Example:
Due to the high price of gasoline, many people are not traveling far this year; they plan to take a **staycation** and stay close to home for their vacation.

American English Expressions

Straight face — showing no emotion.
Example:
He told her with a **straight face** that he was just having lunch with his female co-worker.
He showed no emotion, no laughing, no smiling when he told her that he was just having lunch with his female co-worker. (The implication is that he lied skillfully).

Stupid is as stupid does — if you do stupid things, you are stupid.
Example:
Joe stuck his hand in the fish tank filled with Piranhas.
Stupid is as stupid does.

Take it easy! — don't work too hard! Don't get angry!
See also *Easy does it.*
Examples:
It's my vacation. I'm going to **take it easy**.
I'll see you next week. **Take it easy!**
Sorry I wrecked your Lamborghini. I didn't do it on purpose. **Take it easy!**

Take the ball and run with it — do your job without supervision.
This is based on the game American Football.
Example:
This project is very important. Can you **take the ball and run with it**? Can you do the job without any help, advice, supervision or recognition?

American English Expressions

The latest fad — a passing fancy.
America is possessed by fads. Everyone is obsessed by them, and then they fade away.
Famous fads: Rubik's Cube. Hula hoops. CB radios. Swallowing goldfish. Pet Rocks.
Example:
Is social media **the latest fad**, or is it here to stay?

The real deal — genuine, honest.
Example:
My new boss is **the real deal** – treats the employees fairly and honestly.

There's no there there — that's unsubstantiated, there is no substance to it.
This is a very strange and confusing expression.
An unproven accusation.
Examples:
My candidate has been accused of crookedness and now voter fraud. But **there's** just **no there there**.
You're saying that Joe is a cheater and a thief, but **there's no there there**.

American English Expressions

Think outside the box — solve problems by thinking creatively.
Example:
You've got to **think outside the box** and try to figure out how to make the nuclear reactor safe after the earthquake.

Toast — finished, destroyed.
Example:
During his term of office prices rose and jobs fell, so now he's **toast**.

Touch bases — a very quick update.
This expression comes from the game of Baseball. The runner must touch each base before arriving at Home. The touch can be just for a brief instant, and with a corner of his shoe.
Example:
Let's **touch bases**. We don't have time to discuss this properly, so just tell me briefly if everything is all messed up or not so that I can tell my boss and blame you if something goes wrong.

American English Expressions

Two cents — opinion.
Example:
Joe, what do you think of the match? Can you give us your **two cents**?

Under the weather — not feeling well.
Example:
I'm **under the weather** today, so I'm not going into work. Where are my golf clubs?

Up to no good — been doing nothing good.
Planning something bad.
Example:
I don't trust him. He's **up to no good**.

Walk on water — perform impossible tasks on the job.
See also *Leap tall buildings*.
Example:
We need someone for the job who must be able to **walk on water**. The applicant must be able to work harder and better than most mortals.

American English Expressions

Water cooler — rumor, current opinion.
The supposition behind this expression is that office workers stand around the water cooler and exchange rumor, current opinion, and gossip.
Example:
I overheard at the **water cooler** that the company is going to close this office and move manufacturing to China.

Weigh in — give an opinion.
Example:
Joe, what do you think of the match? Will you **weigh in**?

What goes around comes around — you reap what you sow.
Example:
Joe cheated on his wife Sally with Dora, and he just found out that Dora cheated on him. **What goes around comes around**.

What side your bread is buttered on — be aware of where your best interest lies.
Example:
The politician is not going to anger his special-interest groups — he wants them to continue donating money — he knows **what side his bread is buttered on**.

American English Expressions

Wicked — **extremely. Very much.**
Example:
Man, that Maserati is **wicked** fast.

Wuss out — **lack the courage to do something difficult.**
The U in wUss is pronounced like OO in bOOk.
"Wimp out" is an expression with the same meaning.
Example:
Are we going to climb the mountain? Don't **wuss out**!

Yada yada — **random talking.**
Example:
We got to talking about the weather, and **yada yada**.

You bet! or You betcha! — **I agree. You can bet on it.**
Example:
Have a good weekend, Joe!
You bet!

American English Expressions

You've got two strikes already— one more mistake and you're finished.
Three strikes and you stop playing, for that inning, in the game of baseball.
Example:
The boss said to the worker who came in late two days in a row: "Watch out, **you've got two strikes already.** Come in tomorrow on time or goodbye!"

Zero, zip, zilch— nothing.
(The order of the words is unimportant.)
Every word means "nothing."
See also *Jack* and *Diddly.*
Example:
Did you win anything in the lottery? — Nothing, **zip, zero, zilch!**

American English Expressions

Index

1040, 4
1099, 4
401(k), 4
529, 4
6 figure income, 5
a couple a three, 5
aggravation, 5
aggro, 5
all walks of life, 5
animals that are not confined while they are being raised, 18
annoy, 16
apples and oranges, 5
at the end of the day, 6
back-to-back, 6
bad customer service, 32
bad optics, 6
ball and run with it, 36
ballpark figure, 6
bandwagon, 20
bankruptcy, 11
bases, touch, 38
beam me up Scotty, 7
beginning, 19
begs the question, 7
bet you did, 7
big deal, 27
big whoop, 7
bill of goods, 35
blah blah, 8
blow the whistle, 8
blue state, 8
bone up, 8
brain freeze, 8
brain surgery, 9
bread is buttered on, 40

American English Expressions

brush up, 9
bucket list, 9
bull session, 9
butt dialing, 10
butt out, 10
cakewalk, 10
calm down, 11
came unhinged, 13
can't make this up, 10
carbon footprint, 11
catch as catch can, 11
cell phone dials a number, 10
chapter 11, 11
cheated, 35
chill out, 11
circular reasoning, 7
cloud computing, 12
clueless, 12
cocooning, 12
coed, 12
cold is the new hot, 13
cold turkey, 13
come unhinged, 13
comeback kid, 13
computer glitch, 14
con man, 14
consecutive, 6
cookie-cutter, 14
copay, 14
could care less, 15
couldn't care less, 15
couple a three, 5
crickets, 15
deal-breaker, 15
decision already made, 16
Democratic state, 8

American English Expressions

destroyed, 38
diddly, 15
do not call list, 16
do you mind, 16
doctor or hospital, 30
don't just talk the talk, 16
done deal, 16
drive-by shooting, 17
drop a dime, 17
drunk as a skunk, 17
duck soup, 17
Dutch, 20
easy does it, 18
easy task, 10
easy, 18, 36
eat fast, 23
eating rich foods, 21
embarrassing photos, 6
everything, 24
exam preparation, 8
fad, 37
flirting, unwanted, 22
food for the needy, 18
food pantry, 18
foodie, 18
forget about it, 19
free meals for the homeless, 35
free range, 18
from the get-go, 19
fuhgeddaboutit, 19
game-changer, 19
gang-banger, 19
generation X, 20
generation Y, 20
get on the bandwagon, 20
get-go, 19

American English Expressions

go Dutch, 20
goes around comes around, 40
good luck, 24
good riddance, 21
got your back, 21
gourmet, 18
haphazardly, 11
haul ass, 21
high on the hog, 21
hit the ground running, 21
hitting on, 22
hump day, 22
hump, 23, 28
I bet you did, 7
I could care less, 15
I couldn't care less, 15
I wouldn't put it past him, 22
I'm good, 22
I'm like totally there, 22
ice cream headache, 8
income tax declaration form, 4
incredible, 10
inhale food, 23
it is what it is, 23
jack, 23
John Hancock, 23
jumped the shark, 23
just sayin, 24
kitchen sink, 24
labor of love, 24
latest fad, 37
leap tall buildings, 25
learning curve, 25
list, do not call, 16
living a rich life, 21
long-winded discussion, 9

American English Expressions

lose control of one's emotions, 13
luck out, 25
man up, 25
meh, 25
member of a criminal gang, 19
memory lapse, 33
mind your business, 26
mirror image, 26
my bad, 26
never mind, 26
nitty-gritty, 27
no big deal, 27
no good, 39
no-brainer, 27
nothing, 23, 42
off the top of your head, 27
on a roll, 28
on steroids, 28
on-the-job-training, 28
opinion, 39, 40
out there, 28
outside the box, 38
over the hump, 28
overriding condition that makes all other conditions irrelevant, 19
pencil in, 29
phone call, 10, 17
photos, embarrassing, 6
pie hole, 29
piece of cake, 29
piping hot, 29
post mortem, 29
poster child, 30
provider, 30
put it past him, 22
rain date, 30
rank and file, 30

American English Expressions

real deal, 37
red state, 31
relax, 18
repeat that, 32
Republican state, 31
retirement savings plan, 4
reverse 911, 31
rocket science, 31
rummage sale, 31
rumor, 40
run that by me again, 32
run-around, 32
running late, 32
savings plan to pay college expenses, 4
schedule C, 33
sea change, 33
senior moment, 33
shoo-in, 33
shooting from a car, 17
signature, 23
silence, 15
simpatico, 34
sitting duck, 34
skin in the game, 34
slowly, 18
snowball in Hell, 34
sold a bill of goods, 35
sound bite, 35
soup kitchen, 35
staycation, 35
staying home, 12
straight face, 36
strange, 28
stupid is as stupid does, 36
suddenly, 13
take it easy, 36

American English Expressions

take the ball and run with it, 36
talk the talk, 16
tax declaration form, 4
the latest fad, 37
the real deal, 37
there there, 37
there's no there there, 37
think outside the box, 38
toast, 38
top of your head, 27
touch bases, 38
two cents, 39
two strikes already, 42
unacceptable condition, 15
unaware, 12
under the weather, 39
unfounded approximation, 6
unhinged, 13
uninformed, 12
up to no good, 39
walk on water, 39
walk the talk, 16
walk the walk, 16
walks of life, 5
water cooler, 40
weather, under the, 36
Wednesday, 20
weigh in, 40
what goes around comes around, 40
what side your bread is buttered on, 40
whistleblower, 8
wicked, 41
wuss out, 41
yada yada, 41
you bet, 41
you betcha, 41

American English Expressions

you've got two strikes already, 42
zero, zip, zilch, 42

American English Expressions

For Further Reading

American English Expressions (This book)
    Popular expressions explained.
    For the student of American English.
    By Gabriel F. Gargiulo   (April 12, 2013)
    Paperback: ISBN-13: 978-1478350996 ISBN-10: 1478350997
    Kindle Edition: ASIN: B008G0R6WG

American English Expressions Translated into Russian
    Popular American expressions explained in Russian.
    For the Russian-speaking student of American English.
    By Elena Shishkina and Gabriel F. Gargiulo
    (December, 2013)
    Paperback: ISBN-13: 978-1491278420 ISBN-10: 1491278420

English Lessons with Practice Exercises
    Examples and exercises in grammar
    and pronunciation.
    Student book for ESL learners and teachers.
    By Gabriel F. Gargiulo   (April 1, 2014)
    ISBN-13: 978-1495996603
    ISBN-10: 1495996603

French Expressions
    Popular French expressions explained.
    By Gabriel F. Gargiulo   (June 9, 2013)
    ISBN-13: 978-1489573476
    ISBN-10: 148957347X
    Kindle Edition: ASIN: B008UDGCZ6

American English Expressions

Sharpen your Italian in 50 Days, One Word a Day
By Barbara Agazzi-Poncia and Gabriel F. Gargiulo
Kindle Edition: ASIN: B008DZ2VMO (June 21, 2012)

Miranda Rights in Spanish
The warning read to suspects, in Spanish and English with pronunciation guide.
By Gabriel F. Gargiulo
Kindle Edition: ASIN: B008MZN9Y4 (July 18, 2012)

Idiotismes, locutions, et expressions américains
Popular American expressions explained.
(French Edition)
By Gabriel F. Gargiulo
In French.
Kindle Edition: ASIN: B008PX0SWO (July 26, 2012)

ToUniteAmerica.com
Website for language learners.
Reviews of books for learning languages.
Links to sites for language tutorials and courses
Radio and radio and TV in foreign languages.

Revised July 4, 2013, 22

Made in the USA
Charleston, SC
30 October 2014